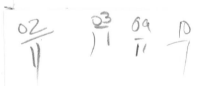

ROBERT E. LEE

David C. King

BLACKBIRCH PRESS, INC.

WOODBRIDGE, CONNECTICUT

Published by Blackbirch Press, Inc.
260 Amity Road
Woodbridge, CT 06525
Web site: http://www.blackbirch.com
e-mail: staff@blackbirch.com
© 2001 Blackbirch Press, Inc.

Printed in China

10 9 8 7 6 5 4 3 2 1

Library of Congress Cataloging-in-Publication Data
King, David C.
Robert E. Lee / by David C. King
        p. cm. — (The Civil War)
Includes index.
        ISBN 1-56711-554-3
1. Lee, Robert E. (Robert Edward), 1807–1870—Juvenile literature.
2. Generals—Confederate States of America—Biography—Juvenile literature.
3. Confederate States of America. Army—Biography—Juvenile literature.
4. Unite States—History—Civil War, 1861-1865—Campaigns—Juvenile
literature. [1. Lee, Robert E. (Robert Edward), 1807–1870. 2. Generals.
3. Confederate States of America. 4. United States—History—Civil War,
1861–1865.] I. Title. II. Civil War (Blackbirch Press)
E467.1.L4 K56 2001
973.7'3'092—dc21   2001002717

CONTENTS

PREFACE: THE CIVIL WAR

Nearly 150 years after the final shots were fired, the Civil War remains one of the key events in U. S. history. The enormous loss of life alone makes it tragically unique: More Americans died in Civil War battles than in all other American wars combined. More Americans fell at the Battle of Gettysburg than during any battle in American military history. And, in one day at the Battle of Antietam, more Americans were killed and wounded than in any other day in American history.

Slaves did the backbreaking work on Southern plantations.

As tragic as the loss of life was, however, it is the principles over which the war was fought that make it uniquely American. Those beliefs—equality and freedom—are the foundation of American democracy, our basic rights. It was the bitter disagreement about the exact nature of those rights that drove our nation to its bloodiest war.

The disagreements grew in part from the differing economies of the North and South. The warm climate and wide-open areas of the Southern states were ideal for an economy based on agriculture. In the first half of the 19th century, the main cash crop was cotton, grown on large farms called plantations. Slaves, who were brought to the United States from Africa, were forced to do the backbreaking work of planting and harvesting cotton. They also provided the other labor necessary to keep plantations running. Slaves were bought and sold like property, and had been critical to the Southern economy since the first Africans came to America in 1619.

The suffering of African Americans under slavery is one of the great tragedies in American history. And the debate over whether the United States government had the right to forbid slavery—in both Southern states and in new territories—was a dispute that overshadowed the first 80 years of our history.

For many Northerners, the question of slavery was one of morality and not economics. Because the Northern economy was based on manufacturing rather than agriculture, there was little need for slave labor. The primary economic need of Northern states was a protective tax known as a tariff that would make imported goods more expensive than goods made in the North. Tariffs forced Southerners to buy Northern goods and made them economically dependent on the North, a fact that led to deep resentment among Southerners.

Economic control did not matter to the anti-slavery Northerners known as abolitionists. Their conflict with the South was over slavery. The idea that the federal government could outlaw slavery was perfectly reasonable. After all, abolitionists contended, our nation was founded on the idea that all people are created equal. How could slavery exist in such a country?

For the Southern states that joined the Confederacy, the freedom from unfair taxation and the right to make their

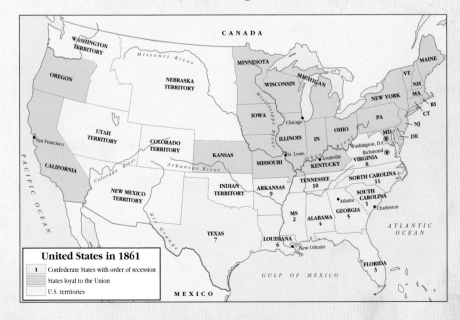

United States in 1861

1   Confederate States with order of secession

    States loyal to the Union

    U.S. territories

own decisions about slavery was as important a principle as equality. For most Southerners, the right of states to decide what is best for its citizens was the most important principle guaranteed in the Constitution.

The conflict over these principles generated sparks throughout the decades leading up to the Civil War. The importance of keeping an equal number of slave and free states in the Union became critical to Southern lawmakers in Congress in those years. In 1820, when Maine and Missouri sought admission to the Union, the question was settled by the Missouri Compromise: Maine was admitted as a free state, Missouri as a slave state, thus maintaining a balance in Congress. The compromise stated that all future territories north of the southern boundary of Missouri would enter the Union as free states, those south of it would be slave states.

In 1854, however, the Kansas-Nebraska Act set the stage for the Civil War. That act repealed the Missouri Compromise and by declaring that the question of slavery should be decided by residents of the territory, set off a rush of pro- and anti-slavery settlers to the new land. Violence between the two sides began almost immediately and soon "Bleeding Kansas" became a tragic chapter in our nation's story.

With Lincoln's election on an anti-slavery platform in 1860, the disagreement over the power of the federal government reached its breaking point. In early 1861, South Carolina became the first state to secede from the Union, followed by Mississippi, Florida, Alabama, Georgia, Louisiana, Virginia, Texas, North Carolina, Tennessee, and Arkansas. Those eleven states became the Confederate States of America. Confederate troops fired the first shots of the Civil War at Fort Sumter, South Carolina, on April 12, 1861. Those shots began a four-year war in which thousands of Americans—Northerners and Southerners—would give, in President Lincoln's words, "the last full measure of devotion."

OPPOSITE: The Confederate attack on Fort Sumter began the Civil War.

Introduction:
The Wrong Train

★ ★ ★ ★ ★

In early spring 1865, more than 35,000 Rebels under the command of General Robert E. Lee had abandoned their defense of Petersburg, the rail center near the Confederate capital at Richmond, Virginia. Outnumbered six-to-one by Ulysses S. Grant's Federal forces, Lee had no choice but to fall back and continue the war further south in North Carolina.

Before first light on April 3, the stately general sat on his horse, Traveller, at a fork in the muddy roads. As the ten-mile-long column of exhausted, starving men moved past, Lee pointed to Amelia, a small town two days' march away. Many troops brushed their hands against Traveller as they slogged past, a sign of affection for the leader they called "Uncle Robert," and of devotion to the Confederate cause.

Few of these battle-hardened Southerners had shoes and most wore tattered rags. Those who did not die along the march were reduced to eating tree bark and leaf buds.

Lee knew rations awaited them in Amelia. Before the retreat, Lee had arranged for supply trains to meet the army. There the men would eat, rest briefly, then travel on to meet the forces of Confederate General Joseph Johnston in North

Carolina. Weary and starved as they were, Lee knew his army would continue the fight as long as they had life in their bodies.

By mid-day, April 4, the Rebels staggered into the sleepy town of Amelia, Virginia, not far from the county seat at Appomattox Court House. Arriving at the rail yard, Lee saw the boxcars and ordered them opened. Inside, instead of food, were cannon shells and ammunition. Not a single ration was in the load—no ham, no bacon, no cornmeal, no milk. There was nothing for his 35,000 starving troops to eat.

Somehow, through a mix-up in the hectic hours before the retreat, the wrong train had been sent to Amelia. The greatest general of the Civil War was speechless, his face a picture of "intense agony." His shoulders sagged. How could he ask his men to continue? How would they have the strength to march 140 miles to the North Carolina border? How could they hold off the Union forces following so close behind? Lee turned to his son, Rooney, an artillery commander. "Keep your command together and in good spirits. Don't let them think of surrender," Lee said. Then he added, "I will get you out of this."

Chapter 1

THE RELUCTANT SOLDIER

Although Robert E. Lee is considered one of the greatest military leaders in American history, he never felt that he had been born to be a soldier. In fact, later in life he often said that choosing a military career was the greatest mistake of his life. In spite of that claim, military life seemed a natural choice for him.

OPPOSITE: General Robert E. Lee became the South's greatest military leader.

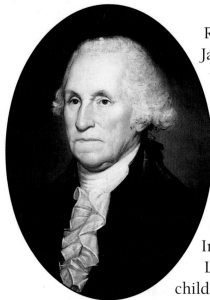

George Washington was young Lee's hero.

Robert Edward Lee, born January 19, 1807, was the youngest son of Henry "Light Horse Harry" Lee, a cavalry officer who had been one of the heroes of the American Revolution and a close friend of George Washington. Two of Robert's ancestors had signed the Declaration of Independence.

Lee's greatest hero from early childhood was his father's friend, George Washington, who had died only a few years before Robert was born. To Lee, the "father of our country" was a personal role model as well as his ideal as a military leader. In later years, people would remark on the character traits of decency, formality, and self-control that Washington and Lee shared.

Lee's father, however, never lived up to the heroism of his cavalry days. He became obsessed with land speculation—buying land cheaply and then selling it for a large profit. Unfortunately, Light Horse Harry was a poor businessman and, like an addicted gambler, ran through his family's savings. While Robert was an infant, his father spent time in debtor's prison. Released, he fled to Baltimore—to escape those to whom he owed money—and was nearly killed in a riot over politics. He left the United States in 1813 to recover his health in the West Indies, and Robert never saw him again.

Light Horse Harry Lee died when Robert was twelve and his older brothers were away at college. Robert became the "man of the house," caring for his mother and younger sister. Robert's mother, Ann Carter Lee, came from one of Virginia's oldest families, and lived on the trust fund that was left to her. As years went by, that fund became smaller, and the family was forced to live in a small house in downtown Richmond, Virginia, rather than a country estate.

It may have been her influence that contributed to Robert's kindness and gentleness, as well as the thoroughness in everything he did. Whatever the source of his personality, Robert was an exceptional young man. His mother suffered health problems throughout her life, and Robert tended to her every need. On cold winter days when he took her for carriage rides, he stuffed papers in the cracks between the wood carriage pieces so his mother would not get a draft.

As a teenager, Robert did not plan on a military career. He wanted to attend Harvard as his older brother had. By the time his college years came around, however, the Lees had fallen on hard financial times. There was no money for Harvard. The family's connections provided Robert with five letters of support from members of Congress for his application to the United States Military

13

Academy at West Point, New York, in 1825. When he left home, his mother said, "How will I ever survive without Robert? He was everything to me."

Lee's record at West Point was another indication that he seemed born to be a soldier. He finished second in his class and had the unique distinction of never receiving a single demerit for violating a rule. Throughout his life, Lee was shy and reserved. At West Point, this meant that he did not mix with other cadets and made few friends. This personal distance, combined with his academic record, might indicate that Lee was one of the most unpopular cadets at the academy. Yet just the opposite was the case. His fellow cadets almost held him in awe. One fellow cadet wrote, "All his accomplishments and alluring virtues appeared natural to him, and he was free from the anxiety, distrust, and awkwardness that attend a sense of inferiority."

★

In 1829, future president Andrew Johnson was elected to his first public office in Greeneville, Tennessee, at age twenty-one.

★

Three important events occurred in 1829 that marked the course of Lee's life. He graduated from West Point, receiving his commission in the Army Corps of Engineers — an elite group that attracted the best cadets. In that combination of triumph and tragedy that seemed to characterize Lee's life, 1829 was also the year that his mother died. He was jolted by the loss. Four decades later, he would write, "It seems now but yesterday."

The third significant event in his life that year was that Lieutenant Lee began courting Mary

Robert E. Lee

Mary Ann Randolph Custis was the daughter of George Washington's adopted son.

Anne Randolph Custis, a young debutante he had known most of his life. Mary was also a member of an old, respected Virginia family—her father was the adopted son of George Washington and was the owner of Arlington, a grand estate overlooking the nation's capital.

Mary's father liked the young lieutenant, but he was not eager to have her marry a junior officer who was landless and practically penniless. He did not stand in the way, however, and Lieutenant Robert E. Lee and Mary became husband and wife on June 30, 1831. In some ways, the union was a

West Point

West Point, New York, is the oldest continuously occupied military post in the United States. It sits on a rocky plateau on the western bank of the Hudson River with a commanding view south toward New York City. During the American Revolution, when much of the fighting took place in New York and New England, the Hudson was a vital supply route. Thus, control of the river was crucial to both Americans and the British. In fact, General George Washington thought West Point was the most important military position in America and established his headquarters there in 1779. To prevent British ships from sailing up the Hudson, American troops built forts there and extended a 150-ton iron chain across the river.

In the late 1700s, soldiers and legislators agreed to create an institution devoted to the science of warfare. President Thomas Jefferson signed legislation establishing the United States Military Academy in 1802. By the time Ulysses Grant went to West Point in 1839, the military academy was graduating classes of between forty and fifty young lieutenants every year. When the Civil War began, a large number of West Point graduates were given commands in the Union Army—or they resigned Union commands to take commands in the Confederate Army. Among the well-known Civil War figures who graduated from West Point and fought on the Confederate side were Confederate President Jefferson Davis; and Confederate Generals Robert E. Lee, Stonewall Jackson, and Joseph Johnston. Union generals, in addition to Grant, included William Sherman, George Meade, and George Thomas—the "Rock of Chickamauga."

One class that made an especially large contribution to the war was the Class of 1846. Known primarily as the class that included the great Stonewall Jackson, twenty of the fifty-nine graduates in 1846 served as generals in the Civil War, though none rose as high in achievement or respect as Jackson. Amazingly, in every major battle Jackson fought in the Civil War, he faced at least one former classmate, including his former roommate, George Stoneman, who commanded the Union cavalry in the battle in which Jackson was killed. The class included George Pickett, leader of the ill-fated charge at Gettysburg, and George B. McClellan, whom Jackson faced in Virginia and at Antietam.

Every Civil War battle had significance for West Pointers. Of sixty major battles fought in the Civil War, fifty-five had West Point graduates on both sides of the conflict. In the remaining battles, a West Point graduate commanded one side or the other.

match of opposites. Robert had grown up in financial difficulty; Mary was wealthy and spoiled by her parents. Robert was shy and reserved; Mary was talkative and enjoyed parties.

Despite their differences, the newlyweds both held strong antislavery feelings. Thus the events that took place nearby during the first summer of their marriage must have shaken them deeply. While the newlyweds set up a home in the Virginia countryside, the state was sent into a panic by a slave revolt. On August 21, a slave named Nat Turner and six other slaves met to make plans for a violent revolt in the tidewater area of Virginia, about eighty miles south of Lee's home.

At 2:00 A.M., Turner and his men entered the home of his master, where they killed the entire family as they slept. They continued on, killing any white people they came upon. Turner's force soon grew to more than forty slaves, most on horseback. By mid-day on August 22, word of the rebellion had reached whites who formed an armed militia. Soon, Turner's force scattered.

In the end, the slaves had stabbed, shot, and clubbed sixty white people to death. After hiding for several weeks, Turner was finally captured on October 30. He was hanged, and then skinned, on November 11. In all, Virginia executed fifty-five people for the revolt. In the panic that resulted from the event, close to 200 African-Americans, including many who had nothing to do with the rebellion, were murdered by white mobs. The

Robert E. Lee poses with his son Custis. Lee's three sons all entered the Civil War, and two became generals.

state legislature of Virginia considered abolishing slavery, but decided instead to retain slavery and to support the strictest policies toward all African Americans.

A Large Family

Robert and Mary Lee would have seven children. She was not a vigorous person and the strain of giving birth to and raising seven children must have been hard on her. In 1835, an illness left her partially lame and often bedridden. Still, the Lees did seem to have a contented family life and the children certainly felt close to their father. His three sons, Custis (born in 1832), Fitzhugh (1837), and Robert (1843) all entered the Confederate Army during the Civil War and two became generals. None of their four daughters ever married, and this may have been because they were never able to find young men who measured up to their image of their father. Several years after Lee's death, Mildred, the youngest, wrote, "To me he seems a Hero, and all other men small in comparison."

For the first seventeen years of his military career, Lee served in a series of posts as an engineer, working to strengthen the nation's harbor defenses or surveying boundaries. In the rapidly-growing Mississippi River port of St. Louis, Missouri, Lee supervised an army group that diverted the flow of the mighty river, allowing larger ships to dock there.

While he enjoyed the precision and order of his work, as well as its creative aspects, he hated life in military posts. So did Mary. She tried it once—and only once—before returning to the comfort of her parents' home—Arlington House—which she had inherited after their deaths. Several times, Lee took a tour of duty at the army engineering office in Washington, D.C., in order to spend more time with his family. The frustration of government work in the nation's capital across the Potomac River, however, led him to request a transfer.

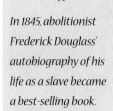

In 1845, abolitionist Frederick Douglass' autobiography of his life as a slave became a best-selling book.

Hero of the Mexican War

Lee planned to leave the army to become a planter shortly before the Mexican War broke out in 1846. The war had been brewing since Texas had gained its independence from Mexico in 1838. For several years, the state had been an independent republic of Americans. The disagreement over Texas' border with Mexico helped bring the U.S. into a war.

The war also came about because of a widely held belief at the time. During the 1840s, many Americans believed strongly in the idea of Manifest Destiny, which claimed that the United States was a unique democracy and had the special right to occupy the entire continent. Acting on this belief meant, for example, removing Native Americans from their traditional lands so white Americans could settle there.

21

In 1845, Manifest Destiny led the United States to annex—or add—Texas as a state. Mexico considered this an act of war. When Mexico objected to the southern border of the new state, many Americans felt that the country to our south should be taught a lesson. Some even went so far as to suggest that Mexico become part of the United States.

Lee reported to Brigadier General John E. Wool in San Antonio, Texas. At nearly forty years old, this would be Lee's first taste of combat. He spent the first months of the war, however, searching for an enemy force that was not eager to take on the U.S. Army. In January 1847, General Winfield Scott asked to have Lee transferred to his staff—which turned out to be a great stroke of luck for Captain Lee. Scott had wanted him to plan artillery placements for his attack on Vera Cruz. Lee's planning turned out to be perfect and was an important factor in several battles. In addition, fellow officers were impressed by how calmly he carried out his assignments under fire.

After a three-day bombardment, Vera Cruz fell and Scott's army next faced a strong Mexican position at Cerro Gordo—a mountain pass. Lee was sent to scout the area, to offer strategic suggestions to General Scott, and then led an assaulting force that overwhelmed the enemy defenses.

Scott gave Lee special mention in his dispatches and he was promoted to major.

Next, Lee supervised the bombardment of Chapultepec, where he was slightly wounded. He was again promoted, this time to lieutenant colonel, then colonel. After the war, he remained in Mexico until May 1848, supervising the creation of accurate maps. General Scott said afterward that Lee was a "military genius" and called him "the very best soldier I ever saw in the field."

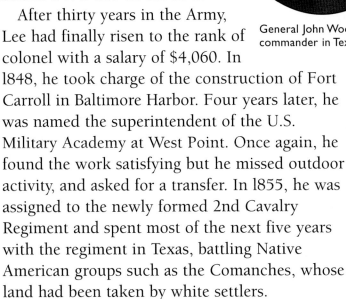

General John Wool, Lee's commander in Texas.

After thirty years in the Army, Lee had finally risen to the rank of colonel with a salary of $4,060. In 1848, he took charge of the construction of Fort Carroll in Baltimore Harbor. Four years later, he was named the superintendent of the U.S. Military Academy at West Point. Once again, he found the work satisfying but he missed outdoor activity, and asked for a transfer. In 1855, he was assigned to the newly formed 2nd Cavalry Regiment and spent most of the next five years with the regiment in Texas, battling Native American groups such as the Comanches, whose land had been taken by white settlers.

While Lee was fighting Comanches on the prairies of Texas, violence of a different kind was breaking out only a few hundred miles north, on the plains of Kansas. It was violence that in many ways would serve as a preview of the Civil War.

"Bleeding Kansas"

In 1854, Senator David R. Atchison of Missouri sponsored a bill that divided the enormous Nebraska Territory into two regions, Kansas and Nebraska. Doing so, Atchison and others believed, would permit the region's eventual entry into the Union as two separate states, one "slave" and one "free." The problem with this stand, however, was that both the Nebraska and Kansas were located north of the southern border of Missouri. More than thirty years before, the Missouri Compromise had banned slavery in new territories north of that line.

Northern lawmakers and abolitionists wanted the Missouri Compromise upheld, thus outlawing slavery in the new territories. The South, however, wanted the Missouri Compromise repealed. It recognized that unless the Compromise was overturned, slave states would gradually become outnumbered because most of the new territory in the growing country was north of Missouri's southern boundary. Eventually, the balance of power would shift and slavery would be prohibited everywhere.

Until the Missouri Compromise was overturned, Southern lawmakers prevented the organization of new territories. They also insisted on rights to slave ownership in any new territory,

24

to do everything to secure those rights, and, if unsuccessful, to dissolve the Union.

The debate of the Kansas-Nebraska Act was at a standstill until an amendment was added that overruled the Missouri Compromise and replaced it with the law from the Compromise of 1850. That law stated that the question of slavery would be settled by a vote of the residents of the territory rather than by the federal government.

The Kansas-Nebraska bill, signed into law on May 30, 1854, was a huge success for the South. Northerners, on the other hand, viewed the act as a betrayal and refused to accept it. Instead, many threw their support behind a new political party, the Republican Party, which strongly opposed slavery.

The Kansas-Nebraska bill also laid out the rules for setting up the first election and gave every advantage to slaveholders and supporters. The Fugitive Slave Laws of 1850 were in effect in the territory before the vote, meaning that anti-slavery people there who helped slaves escape could themselves be jailed and thus unable to vote. Many anti-slavery voters, such as U.S. soldiers, who made up much of Kansas' population, were specifically excluded from the vote.

As events unfolded, pro-slavery forces led a campaign of violence and terror in an effort to make Kansas a slave state. To fight this campaign, abolitionist John Brown brought bands of

25

anti-slavery fighters to Kansas to combat the threat. During a raid of on pro-slavery supporters at Pottawatomie, Kansas, Brown's men massacred five men. Shortly thereafter, an attack by pro-slavery forces left one man dead in Lawrence, Kansas. Throughout 1855 and 1856, the forces for and against slavery continued to fight. The governor of Kansas declared Kansas in a state of open warfare. The area became known as "Bleeding Kansas."

Although he called slavery a "moral and political evil," Lee's views on the actions of abolitionists reflected the views of many Southerners. Lee and his wife had actually freed their slaves in 1856, yet he also spoke out strongly against violent actions of Brown and other abolitionists. In 1856, Lee wrote that "the abolitionist must know that . . . to benefit the slave he must not excite angry feelings in the master. . .still, I fear he will persevere in his evil course." Lee believed that slavery would end in its own due course, and that the interference of abolitionists in matters that did not directly affect them would only lead to war—a result he considered repulsive.

The War Approaches

In the autumn of 1859, Lee happened to be in Washington, D.C., when abolitionists seized the federal arsenal at Harpers Ferry, Virginia. Colonel Lee was ordered to intervene with four companies of local militia and a few United States Marines.

The Harpers Ferry insurrection was led by none other than John Brown who had come to Virginia from Kansas. With an "army" of five African Americans and thirteen whites, Brown planned to capture the weapons at the Federal storehouse and use them to arm slaves throughout the South for a revolution.

Brown's wild revolt did not lead to the general slave revolution he counted on. When Lee arrived with his troops, Brown and his followers were barricaded in a railroad engine house. Lee positioned his men around the building and sent Lieutenant J. E. B. Stuart to negotiate a surrender. When Brown refused to give up, Stuart stepped aside and raised his hat—a signal to storm the building. It was over in minutes. Brown was arrested and, within six weeks, was tried, convicted, and executed.

Most people in the North were shocked by Brown's methods, but many sympathized with his anti-slavery views. He became a hero to many abolitionists throughout the North. To Southerners, however, Brown's raid was a sign of what was to come. It made them more determined to resist the efforts of Northern Republicans to prevent the extension of slavery into the Western territories.

When Abraham Lincoln was elected president in November 1860, and talk of secession spread through the South, Lee observed events with increasing concern. "The South seems to be in a

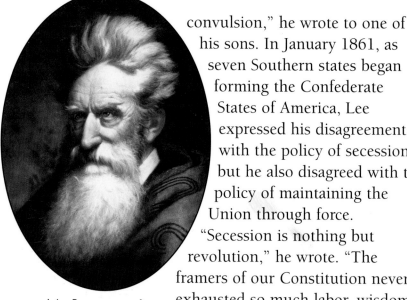

convulsion," he wrote to one of his sons. In January 1861, as seven Southern states began forming the Confederate States of America, Lee expressed his disagreement with the policy of secession, but he also disagreed with the policy of maintaining the Union through force.
"Secession is nothing but revolution," he wrote. "The framers of our Constitution never

John Brown was a fiery opponent of slavery.

exhausted so much labor, wisdom and forbearance in its formation, and surrounded it with so many guards and securities, if it was intended to be broken by every member of the Confederacy at will. Still, a Union that can only be maintained by swords and bayonets, and in which strife and civil war are to take the place of brotherly love and kindness, has no charm for me."

For Lee, as for many other Americans of the time, the bonds he felt for his birthplace and his state were the determining factors in his decision. Like fellow Virginian Thomas Jefferson, the third president, Lee often referred to the state as "my country." It was the oldest colony and the home of four of the first five presidents. Lee was descended from one of the first families to settle the land. When he learned that Virginia had voted to secede, Lee knew he could not wage war against the state: "I cannot raise my hand against my birthplace, my home, my children."

On the day Virginia left the Union, Lee received an offer from President Lincoln to take command of all Union armies. He turned down the offer and, instead, resigned his commission. In a note to Lee, General Winfield Scott wrote, "You have made the greatest mistake of your life, but I feared it would be so."

Abraham Lincoln offered command of all Union armies to Lee.

Five days later, Lee accepted appointment as commander-in-chief of Virginia's military forces and was given the rank of brigadier general. In a touching appeal to his sister Ann, who remained loyal to the Union, he wrote, "I know you will blame me; but you must think as kindly of me as you can, and believe that I have endeavored to do what I thought right."

Lee left Arlington for the ride to Richmond. He would never see his great house again. The Federals quickly took it over. The extensive grounds were used for the burial of Union soldiers during the war, and it later became Arlington National Cemetery.

Chapter 2

At the time the state of Virginia was voting to secede, the Civil War began. At 4:30 A.M. on April 12, 1861, Confederate batteries in Charleston harbor, South Carolina, opened fire on Fort Sumter—still in Federal hands. No one expected a long war. Lincoln called for only 75,000 volunteers to put down the "rebellion." On their side, the Rebels figured that all they had to do was to protect their own territory until the Northerners grew tired of fighting and agreed to let go of the eleven states of the Confederacy.

OPPOSITE: A painting of Rebel soldiers preparing to ford a river. Early in the war, their arms, equipment, and fighting spirit were excellent.

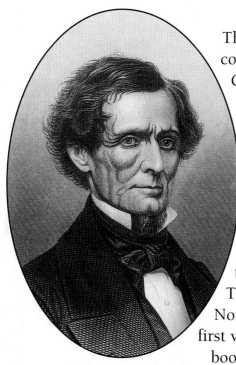

The only way the "Yanks" could beat them, the Confederates believed, was to invade the South and conquer it. The Union made its first try at doing that in July 1861, when a poorly trained army of 30,000 collided with a Confederate force at the Bull Run River, near the town of Manassas, Virginia. The Rebels routed the Northerners, giving them the first victory of the war and a great boost in confidence.

Lee, however, was not part of that battle. Instead, he had been ordered to organize and train 40,000 Virginia volunteers. Late in July 1861, Confederate President Jefferson Davis gave General Lee his first assignment, sending him into western Virginia where the six western counties refused to accept secession. Instead, with the support of Union troops, they hoped to form a new state—West Virginia—and apply for admission to the Union as a free state. Lee's assignment was to work with local militia officers to drive out the Union troops.

Lee's efforts were a complete and humiliating failure. The officers refused to cooperate with one

Jefferson Davis:
President of the Confederacy

In the dramatic story of the Civil War, President Jefferson Davis, who led the Confederate States of America, is sometimes overlooked.

Like Robert E. Lee, Davis attended West Point, though he was not the model cadet. Davis finished twenty-third in a class of thirty-three and received numerous demerits.

After fighting in the Black Hawk War, Davis left the military and took over his brother's plantation outside of Vicksburg, Mississippi. He was a firm believer in the "peculiar institution" of slavery, but treated his slaves kindly. He did not allow whipping, refused to break up families, and took care of sick and elderly slaves.

Davis served as a commander of Mississippi volunteers in the Mexican War and emerged a hero. His fame led to his election to the U.S. Senate from Mississippi where he became a fierce defender of slavery and state's rights.

In 1854, Davis became the Secretary of War under President Franklin Pierce. Re-elected to Senate as the Civil War approached, Davis was a popular choice for Confederate president when fighting broke out. As the war ended and the South was in flames, Davis insisted on prolonging the fighting and ordered Rebel troops to continue with hit-and-run guerilla warfare rather than surrender. Generals Robert E. Lee and Joseph Johnston refused to follow Davis' orders. Davis was captured by Union cavalry in May 1865, and spent two years in prison awaiting trial for treason. Freed on bail in 1867, he was pardoned by President Andrew Johnson and returned to his plantation where he died in 1889.

General Joseph Johnston (above) and Lee clashed at first, but became close allies by the end of the war.

another, late summer rains destroyed the Confederate timing, and Lee's plan for a surprise attack on Union positions developed so slowly that there was no surprise. The battles were not costly in terms of casualties, but the Northern force held firm and what became the state of West Virginia would never be part of the Confederacy.

Because Lee had not seemed aggressive, the Virginia newspapers labeled him "Granny Lee." In the conclusion of a scathing editorial, one editor wrote: "The most remarkable circumstance of this campaign was that it was conducted by a general who had never fought a battle . . . and whose extreme tenderness of blood induced him to [seek] the . . . victory without loss of life."

President Davis still had confidence in Lee. Instead of a field command, however, Davis sent Lee to establish defenses for the coastal area of South Carolina, Georgia, and eastern Florida. "This will be," Lee wrote to his daughter Mildred, "another forlorn hope expedition. Worse than western Virginia."

34

General Lee spent the next six months in what clearly seemed like banishment to him. But the time away from all the action helped Lee develop his strategy for waging the war. In examining his coastal region, he could see clearly that with only 20,000 men available to him, it would be hard to defend long stretches of that coastline. This, in turn, made him realize that the entire Confederacy faced a similar problem: Southern armies were too small and widely scattered to defend so much territory against overwhelming numbers.

Lee's solution: defend the South by making use of surprise and swift movement. It was a strategy similar to that used during the Revolution by American fighters against the overwhelming force of the British. A Rebel army could concentrate its forces on one enemy threat, eliminate it, then decide on the next target.

Lee's strategy was bold and it was workable—certainly more workable than the South's strategy at the time of waiting behind its defensive lines to see what the North would do. What he needed now was a chance to put it into operation.

In March 1862, Lee was called back to Richmond to oversee Confederate military operations under the "direction" of Jefferson Davis. He was, in effect, Davis's personal military adviser, but he could at least influence the decisions made. He found, however, that he often came into conflict with General Joseph E.

Confederate General Richard
Ewell served under Lee.

Johnston, who was in charge of defending Richmond, Virginia, the capital of the Confederacy. Johnston and his army of 40,000 men faced the North's Army of the Potomac, of more than 100,000 men, who were under General George McClellan's command. Two other Confederate armies were in Virginia's Shenandoah Valley—one under Stonewall Jackson, the other under General Richard S. Ewell. Both forces were outnumbered by three Federal armies arrayed against them.

Through the spring of 1862, McClellan's huge army inched closer to Richmond. He had moved his army to the Yorktown peninsula by steamboats and was heading toward the capital from the south while the other three Union armies hoped to press the city from the north. Lee realized that if the Confederate forces remained stationary—on the defensive—it was only a matter of time before they would be overwhelmed. He had Jackson prepare to unite with Ewell and together strike one Federal force. The plan

Robert E. Lee

worked. Both Jackson and Ewell, but especially Jackson, understood perfectly this idea of defense by going on offense. Two Union armies were forced to retreat, giving up the goal of helping McClellan.

At the same time, Johnston's army, after retreating to within eight miles of Richmond, launched a counter-attack. After a promising beginning, the Rebel attack bogged down when Johnston was carried to the rear with two serious wounds. The Confederate president immediately placed Lee in command of the army, which he renamed the Army of Northern Virginia.

The Seven Days

Lee could now plan what became a four-pronged attack against the Federal forces that threatened Richmond. He planned to leave a small force of 20,000 troops in the trenches defending the city. He would then use divisions headed by Generals James Longstreet, Daniel H. Hill, and Ambrose P. Hill to attack after Jackson's troops swooped down from the Shenandoah Valley onto the Union's right flank.

The attack was planned for noon on June 26, 1862. For reasons that were never explained, however, Jackson was several hours late and this ruined the timing for the other generals. When A. P. Hill did not hear from Jackson, he attacked anyhow. As Federal artillery slammed into Hill's infantry, Lee felt he had to order Longstreet and

D. H. Hill to support the assault. Without the initial shock of Jackson's attack on their flank, the Federals managed to withstand the frontal assault. They retreated during the night when they discovered Jackson's approach.

The next few days were similar. Lee's generals never gained the precise coordination for moving huge forces, which was vital. In a series of conflicts that became known as "The Seven Days," McClellan was forced to go on the defensive, but the Rebels could not clinch a decisive victory. In fact, on the last day, July 1, a frustrated Lee ordered a frontal attack into the powerful Union cannons. Thousands of Confederate troops were killed and wounded in a useless effort, and McClellan was able to complete his withdrawal. He had failed to take Richmond, but his army was intact, waiting on the banks of the James River to be ferried back to Washington.

The Seven Days campaign turned out to be costly. The Confederates suffered 20,141 casualties—killed, wounded and missing—a number that equaled 24 percent of their 80,500 men. The Union casualty percentage was considerably lower—15 percent—about 15,900 out of an army estimated at 105,000. But the people of the Confederacy hardly noticed the casualty figures. After weeks of fear with a huge Union army at their gates, Richmond had been saved. General

Robert E. Lee

Lee was no longer "Granny Lee," but the brilliant general who had changed the momentum of the war.

Lee's Classic Warfare

While McClellan's Army of the Potomac remained in striking distance of Richmond, Lee could see the potential for a threat greater than the one they had just met. In late June, Lincoln combined three eastern forces into a new Union "Army of Virginia," commanded by General John Pope. If Pope's force combined with McClellan's army, it would be impossible to fight both at the same time. Once again, Lee's defense was to surprise the enemy by taking the offensive.

Union General John Pope was disliked by his own troops as well as by Confederates.

Trusting from previous experience that McClellan would remain cautious and not try to take Richmond, Lee moved north to the Rappahannock River with 32,000 men. This would hold General Pope's attention long enough for Jackson, with 23,000 troops, to make a forced march to get around the Union flank. The

39

maneuver worked perfectly. Jackson's "foot cavalry" as he called them, moved almost sixty miles in two days, destroyed a huge Federal supply depot, cut the railroad that formed Pope's communications and supply line, then retreated into the dense woods near the old Bull Run battlefield of 1861.

When Pope realized that Jackson's Rebels were now behind his army, he pulled back from the Rappahannock and started a disorganized search for Jackson's force. On August 29, 1862, Pope's army clashed with Stonewall Jackson's much smaller force. This conflict, which became known as Second Bull Run (or Second Manassas) was a standoff the first day, but late in the day Longstreet moved into position at the head of Lee's 32,000-man army. On August 30, Pope attacked Jackson a second time, but Longstreet's artillery and rifle fire crashed into the Federals flank, sending them on a wild retreat.

A Virginia private described the fighting around a Union artillery battery:

> There was a frenzied struggle in the semi-darkness around the guns, so violent and tempestuous, so mad and brain-reeling that to recall it is like fixing the memory of a horrible blood-curdling dream. Everyone was wild with uncontrollable delirium.

The rout of Pope's army couldn't have been more complete. He withdrew all the way to the defenses around Washington, where he was relieved of command and transferred to Minnesota. His battered army was turned over to McClellan. In writing about Second Bull Run, a Union army historian concluded that Pope had been "kicked, cuffed, hustled about, knocked down, run over, and trodden upon as rarely happens in the history of war."

Antietam: The Bloodiest Day

Lee had been in command of the Army of Northern Virginia for three months when he defeated Pope. Before Lee had taken command, the Federals were so confident of victory that they closed their recruiting stations. When he had taken over, McClellan's huge army was hammering at the Confederate trenches just outside Richmond. In the Seven Days battles, Lee's forces fought the Federals to a standstill, although outnumbered almost two to one. Having relieved the pressure on Richmond and put the Union on the defensive, Lee destroyed the second army sent against him at Second Bull Run.

Not surprisingly, he was feeling increasingly at ease as a field commander, and he was developing great confidence in his men. The Rebel troops were awed by his boldness and his firm control. The Confederate high command and the people of the South already saw him as the savior of the Confederacy.

41

In this optimistic atmosphere, Lee decided to carry the war into Northern territory. He was well aware that his men were tired from three months of steady fighting. Many of the men were shoeless. In addition, Lee's army did not have enough artillery or ammunition, and lacked the supply chain that an invasion force needed.

In spite of these difficulties, he felt the opportunity was too good to pass up for several reasons. First, the Union forces were in disarray and the troops demoralized. Second, Maryland was a border state, a slave state still in the Union; a Confederate victory in Maryland might persuade the people there to secede. Third, a victory could convince England and France to recognize the independence of the Confederacy—and perhaps even to offer aid.

In early September 1862, Lee's tattered army crossed the Potomac River into Maryland. A resident watched them coming up the northern banks and wrote that they were:

> *the dirtiest men I ever saw, a most lean and hungry set of wolves. Yet there was a dash about them that the Northern men lacked. They rode like circus riders. Many of them were from the far South and spoke a dialect I could hardly understand.*

A boy, who positioned himself on the river bank, was awed by the huge size of an army on the march:

They came through the town with flags flying and bands playing "Dixie, Dixie," all day long . . . . Day after day an unbroken line passed on due north, and at night the rumble of wagons made sleep impossible for nervous people.

Proud and confident, the Confederates followed Lee's plans carefully. As soon as they crossed the river, the troops separated into four divisions. Three went with Stonewall Jackson to knock out Federal garrisons at Harpers Ferry and Martinsburg in western Virginia. The fourth, under Longstreet, planned to wait for Jackson before proceeding east toward Washington, D.C.

From that time on, nothing went right for Lee's invasion plan. First, there was no welcoming surge of support from the people of Maryland, as Lee had hoped. More serious was the loss of Lee's Special Order 191, which was found in a field by Yankee soldiers, wrapped around three cigars. The paper gave the exact position of each part of Lee's divided force.

McClellan had a perfect opportunity to strike at Lee's divided force, but he delayed for sixteen precious hours—time Lee needed as he waited for Jackson to return from Harpers Ferry. Finally, the Union Army of the Potomac, numbering 88,000 men, moved forward in three columns, an observer wrote, "like a monstrous, blue-black snake, miles long, quilled with the silver slant of muskets. . ."

43

The bridge over Antietam Creek was the scene of vicious fighting during the afternoon of America's bloodiest day.

At South Mountain, a Rebel force under Longstreet and Hill was easily pushed off the high ground at a cost of 2,700 casualties. Lee withdrew to the town of Sharpsburg on September 15 and sent urgent word to Jackson to come at once from Harpers Ferry.

For the next two days, the Army of Northern Virginia tottered on the brink of total destruction. The army's position, at the point where Antietam Creek joins the Potomac River, was not a strong one. With only 20,000 men, it seemed unlikely that the Rebels could hold back McClellan's Federals for long. Even when Jackson arrived with another 12,000 men, the Confederates faced overwhelming odds.

On the morning of September 17, the Union army slammed into the center of the Rebel line.

44

The battle see-sawed through the day, but the Union kept pounding at weak points, until there seemed to be nothing left of the Rebels' center and Lee had no more reserves to pour into the gap. As the Union battle flags edged toward Sharpsburg late in the day, one of the staff officers at McClellan's headquarters recalled it as "one of the most exciting and brilliant exhibitions of he day."

At exactly that moment, a new Rebel force charged into the Union flank, accompanied by the blood curdling "Rebel Yell." It was A. P. Hill's division, arriving after a seventeen-mile forced march from Harpers Ferry. That force was just large enough to push the Federals back toward Antietam Creek, ending the battle in a bloody stalemate. McClellan still had 25,000 men in reserve, but his natural caution prevented him from risking one final assault.

Casualties for the fighting on September 17 were staggering. Confederate losses were an estimated 13,700 casualties to 12,350 Union casualties, making Antietam the bloodiest single day of the war. In fact, no one day in any American war has ever equaled Antietam.

Lee's invasion of the North was over. His Army of Northern Virginia, which had seemed invincible when they stormed across the Potomac, had not lost the Battle of Antietam, but they looked beaten. In an act of defiance, Lee refused to

45

Special Order #191

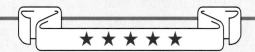

★ ★ ★ ★ ★

No one has ever established exactly how an extra copy of Lee's orders for troop division was made. General D. H. Hill received a copy of Lee's orders, from General Stonewall Jackson, but never knew of a duplicate set of orders. Nor has it ever been explained why the order was left in a field, wrapped around the three cigars. In later years, Hill claimed that it might have been left intentionally by a traitor, but that has never been supported by any evidence.

When McClellan received the order, he began to move much more quickly than usual, but it does not appear that General Lee knew why. Some accounts claim that Lee knew of McClellan's find almost immediately, from a Confederate spy at McClellan's headquarters. Since Lee never mentioned it to any of his associates at the time, this is not likely. This error, which may have changed the course of Lee's invasion and perhaps the war, remains one of the great mysteries of the Civil War.

retreat, as if daring McClellan to order an attack. No attack came, and late the next day the Confederates began to re-cross the Potomac into Virginia. They had lost their momentum and were now on the defensive again.

President Lincoln had been waiting for months for a Union victory in order to issue his Emancipation Proclamation, freeing slaves in certain areas, without having it seem like the desperate measure of a government that was losing. Antietam had stopped the Confederate invasion of Maryland, which he considered enough of a victory to issue the historic statement. The Proclamation stated that as of January 1, 1863, all slaves in states still rebelling against the Union would be free. No slaves would actually be freed until those states surrendered or were occupied by Federal armies.

At first, Lincoln's courageous stand received mixed reactions. Abolitionists were pleased that the president had finally done what they had been demanding for months. Many Northerners were lukewarm, but gradually the feeling emerged that the Union troops were now fighting for a new and noble cause—freedom for 4 million enslaved people.

Chapter 3

BACK ON THE DEFENSIVE

The Battle of Antietam forced Lee back on the defensive—where he was at his best. In his next two major battles—Fredericksburg in December 1862 and Chancellorsville in May 1863—Lee demonstrated his superiority in military tactics.

After crossing the Potomac back into Virginia, Lee prepared his troops to stop a new offensive push by the Army of the Potomac. For several weeks, however, General McClellan moved even more slowly than in the past. President Lincoln's patience finally ran out and he removed the popular general, replacing him with General Ambrose Burnside.

OPPOSITE: Confederate troops at a destroyed railroad bridge in Fredericksburg, Virginia.

Burnside was eager to do the right thing, but he did not feel competent to lead an army of 100,000 troops. He proved his lack of skill by bungling the Battle of Fredericksburg and helping Lee achieve one of the most lopsided victories of the war.

Burnside started out well and quickly had his army ready to cross the Rappahannock River at Fredericksburg, fifty miles north of Richmond. Lincoln had warned his new general to move fast or not at all. Burnside did just the opposite, waiting almost two weeks for pontoon bridges to arrive. This gave Lee time to pull his divisions together and establish a defensive position on the southern edge of Fredericksburg. Once his troops were in position, he hoped that Burnside would attack, and he was not disappointed.

The Confederate defensive line was on a long ridge called Marye's Heights where the soldiers also had the protection of a low brick and stone wall. On December 11, 1862, Rebel signal cannons announced that the Federals had begun crossing the Rappahannock. Looking down on the slope the attackers would have to come up, a Confederate artillery officer commented, "A chicken could not live on that field when we open fire on it."

The officer was correct. The Union troops moved into Fredericksburg without opposition. Burnside then ordered them to attack up the hill

A Confederate wagon was destroyed and several horses were killed by a Union artillery shell outside Fredericksburg.

against Marye's Heights. Rebel cannons and muskets sliced through the advance in minutes, forcing them back down the slope. That first assault should have been enough, but Burnside stubbornly ordered five more attacks. All failed. Watching his jubilant troops celebrate the slaughter, Lee said to Longstreet, "It is well that war is so terrible—we should grow too fond of it."

Union forces lost 12,500 killed and wounded that day to 5,000 Confederates. In writing about the loss, a Union newspaper concluded, "It can hardly be in human nature for men to show more valor, or generals to manifest less judgment."

Burnside kept his army around the Rappahannock for another month. He planned

General Joseph Hooker was wounded at the Battle of Antietam.

another crossing in January 1863, but thirty hours of torrential rain flooded the river and turned the surrounding land into a swamp. As Burnside struggled to get his army back north of the river, one Union officer jokingly sent a requisition for "soldiers twenty-five feet high to work in mud eighteen feet deep."

Lincoln had seen enough and, to Burnside's great relief, removed him from command, replacing him with General Joseph Hooker, known as "Fighting Joe." Hooker was as eager for the assignment as Burnside had been reluctant. "May God have mercy on General Lee," he announced boldly, "for I will have none."

Chancellorsville, May 1863

Throughout Lee's campaigns since The Seven Days, he had relied heavily on two men. One of these was Stonewall Jackson, who seemed to have a special bond with Lee, each understanding the other by intuition. The other man he relied on was Jeb Stuart, the colorful, flamboyant general in command of the Army of Northern Virginia's cavalry. Lee called Stuart "my eyes and ears," and he filled that role perfectly. On several occasions, he had led his cavalry completely around the Army of the Potomac, returning with valuable information on the enemy's movement and strength. In addition, with 18,000 skilled horsemen serving under him, Stuart commanded an extra fast-moving division. Cavalry in the Civil War rarely fought on horseback. Instead, they acted like mobile infantry, dismounting in order to fight.

★

Like Lee, Davis, and Grant, Jackson was a graduate of West Point and served with distinction in the Mexican War.

★

To take on "Fighting Joe" Hooker in the spring of 1863, Lee made use of both Jackson and Stuart. First, in late April, Stuart led his cavalry on an examination of Hooker's advance. Once again, he saw the Army of the Potomac approaching the Rappahannock near Fredericksburg. Stuart returned to the south side of the river where Lee and Jackson sat on crates studying the Union buildup. He reported that Hooker's right flank was "hanging in the air" without a barrier such as a river or woods for protection.

Jackson said he could swing around that flank and attack the Federals from the rear. Lee asked, "What do you intend to make this movement with?" Jackson answered, "With my whole corps."

This was an extraordinary risk by Lee and Jackson. Jackson led 30,000 men on his flanking

53

maneuver, leaving Lee with only 14,000 men to face the main body of Hooker's army. Jackson's corps had to march twelve miles along a narrow road, which forced them to stretch out into a column of nearly 10 miles. Once the head of the column reached its position, it took 5 more hours for the last of the 30,000 men to catch up. By early evening, the maneuver was complete. The men on Hooker's right flank suddenly heard the piercing sounds of the "Rebel Yell" as Jackson's men charged out of the dense woods into the rear of the Army of the Potomac.

This remarkable maneuver led to Confederate victory in the Battle of Chancellorsville—and was widely regarded as Lee's most spectacular triumph. Lee was able to let Jackson take such a

This illustration shows Lee leading his troops at Chancellorsville, one of his greatest victories.

risk because he was so skilled at analyzing the general opposing him. He knew, for example, that Hooker was capable of moving quickly. But he also observed the Federals were building log barriers and entrenchments. This convinced him that Hooker had lost his nerve and was preparing to be on the defensive, at least for a time. Northern critics were outraged that the Union army had once again been out-thought and out-fought by the much smaller Army of Northern Virginia.

Fredericksburg and Chancellorsville had displayed Robert E. Lee at his very best, although the latter triumph had cost him Stonewall Jackson. Wounded by his own men on the night of the great victory, he died a week later.

Chapter 4

THE SOUTH'S GREAT GAMBLE

Despite losses in the first two years of the war, Union forces still felt that time was on their side. After the Confederate victory at Fredericksburg, Lee had commented, "I wish these people would go away and leave us alone." But, of course, the North was not about to leave them alone. The sheer numbers of troops available to the Union commanders continued to grow, while the South was having trouble bringing in fresh recruits. Before Chancellorsville, for example, Lee had been forced to send Longstreet south of Richmond where several small Union divisions had been landed. This left Lee with a total of less than 60,000 men to face the Army of the Potomac which now numbered 135,000.

OPPOSITE: This photograph of Lee was taken during the Civil War. His troops sometimes called him "Uncle Robert."

57

The docks at New Orleans. The Union had control of this vital shipping port by late 1862.

Lee, Jefferson Davis, and the other Confederate leaders knew that events could not continue on the same path. The Union would put more and more men on that road to Richmond, challenging Lee's ability to drive them back.

The fighting in the West was also reaching a crisis point. The two Confederate armies in the West had been trying to hold back Union advances since the war's outbreak. In the middle west, a stalemate had developed in Tennessee, but farther west, General Ulysses S. Grant was beginning to exercise more and more authority. A year earlier, he had given the North its first victories by capturing Forts Henry and Donelson. Now he was closing in on Vicksburg,

Robert E. Lee

Mississippi—a fortress city that held the key to control of the Mississippi River.

The Union navy had used armed steamboats and gunboats to capture New Orleans and the lower stretches of the Mississippi and had helped Union armies gain control of the Northern portions of the river as far south as Vicksburg. The South, however, continued to hold a 250-mile stretch of the river from Vicksburg to Port Gibson. A 30,000-man army under General John C. Pemberton had strong defensive positions in Vicksburg. If Vicksburg fell to Grant's Federals, the Union would control the entire Mississippi, giving them a natural invasion route into the deep South. It would also cut the Confederacy in two, leaving Arkansas, Louisiana, and Texas isolated from the rest of the Confederacy.

General Ulysses Grant became the North's greatest military leader—and Lee's biggest foe.

Deciding on a Strategy

In mid-May, Lee went to Richmond to meet with Davis and his cabinet to plan the South's next move. Confederate leaders were convinced that part of the Army of Northern Virginia should be sent to Mississippi to relieve the pressure on

Robert E. Lee

General Pemberton and his 30,000 men who were now trapped inside the fortress city. Grant had placed the city under siege, with 70,000 troops commanding every land approach and Union gunboats controlling the Mississippi. General Longstreet agreed with this choice of actions.

The Confederate leaders listened as Lee presented his counter-arguments. First, Lee said, it seemed unlikely that he could move his army west fast enough to save Vicksburg. If he tried, the Army of the Potomac would quickly move on Richmond and the loss of the capital would be a devastating blow to the South.

Instead, Lee argued, it was time to launch another invasion of the North. A quick strike into Pennsylvania might force Grant to send part of his army to meet the threat. Even if that didn't happen, the invasion would certainly relieve the pressure on Richmond. At the same time, Lee's army would be able to live off Pennsylvania farms for a time, giving Virginia relief from having to feed so many men and provide forage for their horses and mules. "The question of food," Lee told the gathering, "gives me more trouble and uneasiness than everything else combined."

Lee saw that the Confederate leaders were listening attentively and presented more positive reasons for invading. For one thing, he claimed, a defensive victory was not likely to persuade

England or France to recognize the Confederacy. Carrying the war into the North, however, and winning there could be very convincing.

Another argument in favor of Lee's plan was that, once in Pennsylvania, his men could destroy the bridge over the Susquehanna River at Harrisburg, cutting the main railroad link between the East and the Midwest. "After that," he said with growing optimism, "I can turn my attention to Philadelphia, Baltimore, or Washington as may seem best for our interest."

Finally, Lee was keenly aware that the people of the South and the leaders had enormous confidence in him and his army. He made his final point—the only one he really needed. "There never were such men in an army before," he said. "They will go anywhere and do anything if properly led."

Lee's arguments easily won over the others. James Longstreet remained reluctant, but finally agreed to the plan on the condition that it would be "offensive in strategy but defensive in tactics." In other words, the invasion was offensive but, for the actual fighting, Longstreet wanted it to be defensive—taking a strong position and forcing the Federals to attack them.

★

Longstreet had been a member of U.S. Grant's wedding party.

★

Longstreet was actually making a critical point. Lee's army seemed invincible when they were in a defensive position from which Lee could make his bold and startling offensive moves. The only time the army had been stopped was on the offensive at Antietam.

Because of Jackson's death, Lee had to reorganize his army. He divided his roughly 80,000 Rebels into three corps, each corps containing three infantry divisions. Longstreet remained in command of I Corps and was now the man Lee would turn to most. To replace Jackson, Lee chose Lieutenant General Richard S. Ewell for II Corps. Ewell had fought well in earlier campaigns but he had lost a leg at Second Bull Run. After convalescing for nine months, he was eager to be back in action. At the head of the new III Corps was Lieutenant General A. P. Hill— another skilled fighter but often impatient and given to rash action. In addition, Lee now had four brigades of cavalry, all commanded by General Stuart.

Lee made the command changes on May 30, 1863, and four days later the Army of Northern Virginia was on the move. The spirited Southerners were marching toward the turning point in the war.

The Road to Gettysburg

On June 3, 1863, as General Longstreet's three divisions moved slowly toward Virginia's Blue Ridge Mountains, the men could see General Lee on a low hill near their line of march. This was how they usually saw him—astride Traveller looking calm and confident, the picture of the

South's strength. What the men did not know was that inside the erect figure, heart disease that would eventually kill him was already sending sharp pains through his chest.

Since the Confederates knew nothing of Lee's condition, they set off to invade Pennsylvania with great confidence. The move north was brilliantly planned by Lee. It took Hooker, on the far side of the Rappahannock, several days to discover that the Army of Northern Virginia was even on the move, longer still to guess their destination.

Longstreet's men took up positions in the passes through the Blue Ridge Mountains leading to the Shenandoah Valley. The Shenandoah became the highway by which the corps led by Hill and Ewell marched north into southern Pennsylvania. Since Hooker's men could not get through the passes, they could not tell how many men Lee was sending or how far north they had progressed.

By the middle of June, the Rebel army was stretched out for 100 miles through the Shenandoah Valley, with the lead divisions on the Pennsylvania border. A worried General Hooker sent a telegram to President Lincoln asking if he should cross the Rappahannock and attack Richmond. Lincoln wired back:

> *I think Lee's Army, and not Richmond, is your true objective point. . . . If he comes toward the Upper*

63

Potomac, follow on his flank, and on the inside track. . . . Fight him when opportunity offers."

Hooker did as he was told and began moving his army north on the eastern side of the Blue Ridge Mountains. He carefully kept his force between Lee and Washington, D.C.

As always, Lee planned to rely on General Stuart's cavalry to keep him informed about the Army of the Potomac. When Lee crossed the Potomac and moved into Pennsylvania, Stuart's cavalry

Union General Alfred Pleasanton commanded a Union cavalry division.

division was to move onto Lee's right flank and remain there to protect it. In the Gettysburg campaign, however, Stuart let his commander down for the first time. Some historians are convinced that this failure cost Lee any chance of winning at Gettysburg.

Stuart had started out all right on the move north. His veteran troopers had always been able to ride circles around any cavalry sent against them. But the Federals had been improving their cavalry steadily, and Hooker had formed a new cavalry division commanded by General Alfred Pleasanton. On June 19, Pleasanton's 11,000 men crossed the Rappahannock and caught Stuart and his men completely off guard. The Southern troopers recovered quickly and a fierce battle ensued—the largest cavalry battle of the war.

The battle was a shock to Stuart. The Federals had fought his men on nearly equal terms before pulling back across the river. After suffering 523 casualties (to 866 Federal killed and wounded), he needed time to rest his men and horses. Lee sent word, however, that he could not wait.

The embarrassment of nearly losing a cavalry battle may have convinced Stuart to take an unnecessary risk. A week later, he saw his chance to restore his reputation as invincible. Instead of moving directly to the Potomac River to cross, he decided he could make the crossing nearly as fast by riding completely around the Army of the Potomac. This was one of his favorite maneuvers and would surely win admiration.

Stuart miscalculated. He did not realize how active Hooker's men were or how spread out. He was forced to fight other cavalry skirmishes and was nearly captured in one. The result was that after June 23, Lee had no further word from Stuart for ten crucial days. By the time Stuart caught up, the Battle of Gettysburg was in its last grim hours.

During the same period, the first clash between Rebels and Yankees took place at Winchester, Virginia. Lieutenant General Ewell, commanding his corps from a carriage, gained a measure of revenge for his lost leg by routing a 9,000-man Federal force. After a day and a night of fighting, Ewell's II Corps had taken 3,358 prisoners, inflicted 443 casualties, captured 23 cannons, plus 300 wagons and horses—all at a cost of 269 casualties. Ewell had passed his first test as a corps commander with flying colors.

By now, "Fighting Joe" Hooker had seen enough. He sent a wire to Lincoln confessing that the South's invasion of Pennsylvania "is not in my power to prevent." That convinced the President that Hooker was not up to the task. On June 27, he removed him and replaced him with George Gordon Meade, a tough, quiet officer whom the men respected.

Without Stuart, Lee had no way of knowing about the change of command or where the Army of the Potomac was. By this time, all three of Lee's corps were in Pennsylvania, although still widely scattered. On June 28, a spy working for Longstreet reported that Meade was now in command and that the Army of the Potomac had already crossed the Potomac. He also reported that the entire Union force of 111,000 men was now at Frederick, Maryland, and closing in on Lee's flank.

Lee at first refused to believe the ragged, exhausted spy. He soon realized that the information was accurate and became furious with Stuart for letting him down. Lee had been planning to march on Harrisburg. The approach of Meade's army forced him to change plans. Lee sent emergency messages to all his commanders to head for Gettysburg.

The choice of Gettysburg was inevitable. It was a crossroads town with nine roads running through it. The separate divisions of Lee's army could find roads leading to it. As June ended, the two armies were on a collision course to meet at the peaceful Pennsylvania town.

The Battle of Gettysburg

Gettysburg was the greatest single battle of the Civil War. Many have seen it as the decisive struggle, the war's turning point. It was certainly as dramatic as any battle, with dozens of spectacular moments that have made it the most studied of all Civil War battles and, in many ways, the most heroic.

One of A. P. Hill's divisions was closest to Gettysburg when Lee's urgent message to converge arrived. At the same time, some Rebels learned that there was a shoe factory in Gettysburg, and since some of the men were shoeless, they asked if they could go in and help themselves. Hill gave permission.

As the Rebel division approached the town on the morning of July 1, they saw a line of Union cavalry approaching—a brigade commanded by General John Buford. Buford quickly had his men dismount and open fire from the protection of trees and fences. The Southerners reacted quickly. They outnumbered the Federals three to one but they had trouble pushing the Blues back. One reason for their difficulty was that Buford's men

67

were equipped with new breech-loading rifles. With these carbines, each man could get off 15 to 20 shots a minute to 2 or 3 for the Rebels equipped with standard muzzle-loaders.

Buford's thin blue line held for two hours while he sent an urgent message to his corps commander for reinforcements. The Confederates pushed them all the way through the village. More Confederates arrived just as Union troops from two corps collided with them. The day began with sharp skirmishes that grew larger as troops from both sides arrived. Neither Meade nor Lee was ready for a full-scale battle. They had not planned to fight at Gettysburg, and neither even knew the fighting had begun until it was well under way.

With the shrill Rebel Yell, more men from Ewell's corps plowed into the Federal lines. The 6th Wisconsin, known as the "Iron Brigade," found itself in a familiar position of holding off superior numbers until help arrived. But this time the determined Confederates pressed their advantage. Of 1,829 men in the Iron Brigade at the start of the day, 1,153 became casualties.

The fighting was ferocious as the Northerners fled through the town to make a stand on high ground south. As the Iron Brigade was forced off a hill called Seminary Ridge, an artillery officer recalled,

"For seven or eight minutes ensued probably the most desperate fight ever waged between artillery and infantry

A photograph of Gettysburg in 1863. The quiet town was a crossroads in southern Pennsylvania.

at close range without a particle of cover on either side . . . bullets hissing, humming & whistling everywhere; all crash on crash, and peal on peal, smoke, dust, splinters, blood, wreck and carnage indescribable."

A Union artillery officer, 19-year-old Lieutenant Wilkeson, had his leg nearly severed by a cannon-ball. Lying on a blanket, Wilkeson twisted his officer's sash into a tourniquet, then used his pocket knife to complete amputating the leg.

When Lee arrived late in the day he was angry and said he had not ordered a general engagement. But then he saw the battlefield and realized

69

Lee's headquarters at Gettysburg.

that the opportunity was too good to pass up. He could see that the Federals were barely hanging on to Cemetery Hill. He sent word to Ewell that "It is only necessary to press those people in order to secure possession of the heights."

Ewell, however, made no move. After having such a close relationship with a military genius like Stonewall Jackson, Lee was used to counting on his subordinates knowing what to do. Consequently, his orders often came across more as suggestions than commands. This may have been the case with Ewell. Perhaps he did not recognize that taking the hill would give the South the high ground, forcing the Federals the next day to try to dislodge them.

Before Lee could get to Ewell, however, Union General Winfield Scott Hancock had arrived on Cemetery Hill, boosting the Union morale and stiffening their defense of the hill. As night fell, the North had established a defensive line shaped like a 3.5-mile long fishhook. Cemetery Ridge was the long shank, bending at Cemetery Hill. Little Round Top was the eye of the hook, and Culp's Hill formed the barb.

The Southerners took up their position on Seminary Ridge, with a long, mile-wide valley between them and the enemy. The Rebel soldiers knew how close they had come to completely crushing the Army of the Potomac. They were eager to try again the next day. So was Lee. "The enemy is here," he told his corps commanders. "And we will fight him here. If we do not whip him, he will whip us."

The next day, Longstreet argued with Lee about making a frontal assault on Cemetery Ridge and the other heights. Longstreet suggested moving around Meade's flank, getting between him and Washington, then forcing the Federals to attack them on ground that the South chose. Lee refused to listen, and Longstreet noted later that he seemed out of sorts.

71

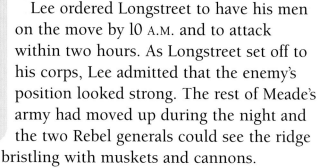

Lee ordered Longstreet to have his men on the move by 10 A.M. and to attack within two hours. As Longstreet set off to his corps, Lee admitted that the enemy's position looked strong. The rest of Meade's army had moved up during the night and the two Rebel generals could see the ridge bristling with muskets and cannons.

It took Longstreet most of the day to get his men in position. Problems did get in the way, but he may have been slow because he opposed the strategy. Late in the day, two of Longstreet's Texas regiments and an Alabama regiment led by Colonel William Oates began an assault on the hill called Little Round Top. Oates had realized that Rebel artillery on that hill would have a clear shot of the entire Union defensive line. As Oates set out to lead his men up the rugged hillside, the hill was unoccupied by either side.

On the Union side, however, Meade's staff officer had also noticed the strategic importance of the hill and ordered two brigades to take control of it. He told Colonel Joshua Chamberlain, commander of the 20th Maine Volunteers, "This is the left of the Union line . . . . You are to hold this position at all costs."

Chamberlain, who had been a professor of speech and modern languages, was determined to hold Little Round Top. In the process, he became one of the heroes of the Battle of Gettysburg.

Robert E. Lee

When the Rebels neared the top of the hill, they were shocked to meet withering fire from the Federals who had just arrived at the crest. The Southerners fell back, Oates ordered them to try again, and then a third and fourth time. Chamberlain later wrote:

Chamberlain, badly wounded at Fredericksburg, won a Medal of Honor at Gettysburg.

> *The edge of the conflict swayed to and fro, with wild whirlpools and eddies. At times I saw around me more of the enemy than of my own men; gaps opening, swallowing, closing again with sharp convulsive energy. All around, a strange, mingled roar. . . . We expended our last cartridges. . . every round was gone. Knowing the supreme importance of holding this ground . . . I saw no other way to save it, or even ourselves, but to charge with the bayonet. . . .*

With a wild yell that rivaled the Rebel Yell, Chamberlain and his men stormed down the steep slope, steel flashing. The stunned Southerners reeled and stumbled down the hill. The battle for Little Round Top was over.

Other regiments in Longstreet's I Corps attacked close to the center of the Federal line where Union General Dan Sickles had moved his division 500 yards ahead of the rest of the Union line. This salient, or bulge, was too tempting for Longstreet's men to resist. Rebel troops smashed into Sickle's men in a fight that turned into bloody hand-to-hand fighting in a rocky gully called the "Devil's Den."

73

Union General Joshua Chamberlain was a colonel at Gettysburg.

Late in the day, some of Longstreet's Rebels reached through to the North's last defensive line on Cemetery Ridge. If they could break through, the Union soldiers would run in wild retreat because there was no one behind them to reinforce that line. Union General Winfield Scott Hancock frantically rushed what men he had to plug one gap after another. In one desperate move he ordered the First Minnesota Regiment into a suicidal countercharge to hold the Confederates until reinforcements could be brought up. The Federals obeyed the command, rushing into sheets of musket and artillery fire, losing 216 out of their 262 men in a matter of minutes. Their sacrifice gave the Union a chance and the line held.

Still, the Confederates refused to give up. "On they came like the fury of a whirlwind," wrote one Union soldier. The Federals crouched behind barricades at the crest of the ridge, held their fire until the order was given, then unleashed the fury of their cannons and muskets, blasting huge holes in the Rebel lines. Each wave of attackers seemed about to crash through and send the Federals into

Robert E. Lee

retreat, but then Union reinforcements would arrive just in time to turn back the charge.

Some 7,000 rebels were killed, wounded, or captured, almost one-third of the 22,000 Rebels Longstreet committed to the attack. In an understatement, the Rebel general said, "We have not been so successful as we wished."

In fact, Lee's army had gained nothing. Meade's defenders still held the ridge as well as Cemetery Hill, Little Round Top, and Culp's Hill.

That night, Meade met with his generals in a farmhouse behind Cemetery Ridge. In two days of fighting, the Union had lost 15,000 men. The generals, however, agreed that they should hold their ground and try to end the battle on the third day.

Lee, too, was determined to fight the next day. For two days his courageous troops had come tantalizingly close to winning it all. Another general might have reasoned that even though the Rebels had come close to breaking through at one point, there was no possibility of dislodging such large numbers from so many entrenched positions. But Lee's entire approach to warfare was to take the offensive, to attack. And that was how his troops faced the final day at Gettysburg.

The third and final day of the Battle of Gettysburg led to one of the most dramatic episodes of the war—"Pickett's Charge." Lee was determined that his army would finally crash through the North's defenses and give the South the victory he so desperately craved. Ewell's men were to attack Meade's right flank and Longstreet's division would assault the center at the same time. At dawn on July 3rd, however, the sound of heavy artillery fire from Ewell's direction indicated that there would be no combined attack. By mid-morning the cannons fell silent. Ewell's men were too battered and exhausted to fight more that day.

Everything now depended on a very reluctant General Longstreet and his I Corps. Lee showed him where his men were to attack—across the shallow valley, a half-mile wide, that separated the South's line on Seminary Ridge and the North's line on Cemetery Ridge. There was no cover in that open space, so the Rebel troops would be exposed to enemy fire the entire way. Longstreet objected vigorously, saying "no 15,000 men . . . can take that position."

Lee refused to change his mind, although he was willing to excuse some of Longstreet's regiments that had taken a beating the day before. The charge would be made by 12,000 men, anchored by a new division of 6,000 men led by General George E. Pickett.

At 1:00 P.M., the mid-summer stillness was shattered by the boom of cannons. Longstreet had pulled together every cannon he could find— more than 140 in all—and unleashed the heaviest artillery fire ever heard on the North American

Robert E. Lee

Pickett's charge was the last desperate attempt by the Confederates to achieve victory at Gettysburg.

continent. He hoped to blast holes through the enemy lines that would give Pickett's men a chance to get across the valley.

Union cannons quickly responded and the valley soon filled with dense gray smoke. Only later did Longstreet and his officers learn that with the artillery officers unable to see in the smoke, most Southern shells sailed over the crest of Cemetery Ridge, landing harmlessly beyond the Federal defenses.

The artillery duel ended after two hours and another tense silence followed. Late afternoon breezes pushed clouds of smoke out of the valley. The time had come to attack. Longstreet could not bring himself to order Pickett's men to charge, but Pickett knew. "I am going to move forward, sir," Pickett said.

On Pickett's signal, 12,000 Confederate soldiers emerged from the woods. They advanced in perfect formation, separated by a only few inches, flags flying, officers on horseback urging them on, reminding the men to hold their fire until they heard the order. Marching at a double-quick pace, it would take them about 17 minutes to cross the valley and start up the slope.

Most never made it that far. Once out in the valley, Federal artillery hit them from the side and head on. Non-exploding cannon balls bounced down the hill at great speed, smashing into clusters of men. Musket fire also came at them from two sides. A Virginia soldier recalled: "Volley after volley of crashing musket balls sweep through the line and mow us down like wheat before the scythe." Another remembered the sounds of that battle as "strange and terrible, a sound that came from thousands of human throats . . . like a vast mournful roar."

With 100 yards to go, the Rebels heard the order to stop and fire. They unleashed a tremendous volley that knocked out an artillery battery and sent hundreds of Yankees in a frenzied retreat. A few hundred Confederates made it to the crest of the ridge and at that moment, many historians agree, the Confederacy reached the point at which the South was closest to achieving victory both in the battle and in the struggle to achieve independence.

The crest of the Confederate wave lasted only a few moments. Federal troops quickly countered and the Rebels on the ridge, without leaders, had a choice of staying and being shot or captured, or trying to get back to their own lines.

Most chose to back down the slope, still defiant, still shooting. Some Union officers tried to launch a counter-attack, but the men ignored the order. They, too, had nothing left to give.

As the battered Rebel force staggered back to the woods, Lee rode among them, offering what encouragement he could. To Longstreet he admitted, "It is all my fault. I thought my men were invincible." Of the nearly 6,000 men in

79

Confederate prisoners after Gettysburg.

Pickett's division, only 800 answered the next day's roll call.

The Battle of Gettysburg was a devastating defeat for Lee and the South. Total Confederate casualties for the three days were about 28,000. In other words, one out of every three men who left Virginia with Lee had been killed, wounded, captured, or listed as missing. Nearly all of those men were tough veterans who could not be replaced. The North had suffered nearly as many casualties but, with its much greater population, replacements were available.

Some historians consider the Battle of Gettysburg the turning point in the war. This is at least partly true in relation to General Lee and his

Robert E. Lee

Army of Northern Virginia.
After Gettysburg, Lee never
again tried to carry the war
to the North. In fact, the
army never again went on
the offensive.

A large number of
Civil War historians
agree that while
Gettysburg was a severe
blow, the mortal blow
came from General
Ulysses S. Grant. On July 4,
1863, as Lee's army began the
long, dangerous journey back
to Virginia, Grant accepted
General Pemberton's surrender of
Vicksburg and his Rebel army of
30,000 men. Within a few days,
Port Gibson fell and the North had control of the
full length of the Mississippi River.

After Gettysburg,
Lee's dream of
victory was crushed.

Meade in the East and Grant in the West could
now advance into Confederate territory with ever-
increasing numbers. The South's armies were
faced with a growing number of desertions. Once
men thought their cause was lost, they wanted to
be home with their families. Weapons and other
supplies were also a problem. The North's naval
blockade of Southern ports made it hard for
blockade runners to get through with arms and
other supplies from Europe.

Chapter 5

The long march back to Virginia was both dangerous and tragic. The wounded were piled into wagons that had no springs for the punishing ride home. Every bump in every wagon was agony for the wounded and sick inside. Lincoln urged Meade to go after them, but Meade remained cautious, even after it became clear that summer rains had swollen the Potomac and it would take the Confederates several days to cross. Meade also knew his men were too exhausted from their three-day struggle—the bloodiest battle of the entire war. On July 14, the Army of Northern Virginia crossed the Potomac.

OPPOSITE: This illustration, from a Union publication, depicts Lee's surrender to Grant. In truth, Lee was several inches taller than Grant.

83

Lee and his troops escaped into Virginia where they hoped to have time to reorganize the battered army. Lee still accepted full responsibility for the defeat and wrote to President Davis, "No blame can be attached to the army for its failure to accomplish what was projected by me, nor should it be censured for the unreasonable expectations of the public. I am alone to blame." He then offered to resign, an offer Davis declined.

In the spring of 1864, Ulysses S. Grant was placed in command of all Union armies and prepared for a major Federal offensive. While Grant was sending his chief lieutenant general, William Sherman, into Georgia, Grant would be with Meade and the Army of the Potomac for the main offensive against Lee and Richmond. In April 1864, Longstreet and his I Corps returned from Tennessee. Lee reviewed the troops, most of whom had not seen him since Gettysburg. One of Longstreet's men wrote:

> "The men seemed satisfied to lay their hands on his gray horse or to touch the bridle, or the stirrup, or the old general's leg—anything that Lee had was sacred to us fellows who had just come back. And the General—he could not help from breaking down. Tears traced down his cheeks, and he felt that we were again to do his bidding.

Grant's campaign to end the war began in May 1864, when the Army of the Potomac—120,000

strong—crossed the Rapidan River to take on the
Army of Northern Virginia with about 65,000
men. Grant planned to pursue Lee relentlessly.
When a battle ended, there would be no rest. Win
or lose, Grant would press forward. In time, Lee's
army would be worn down. With few
recruits to replace losses, the Army of
Northern Virginia would eventually
cease to be a fighting force.

Meantime, General William
Tecumseh Sherman, was taking
on the western Confederate
army under General Joe
Johnston. Sherman intended to
invade Georgia, capture the
major city of Atlanta, then make a
destructive march through Georgia
to the sea. Beginning in May 1864, it
would take until September to take
Atlanta against fierce Rebel resist-
ance. Sherman's army suffered
27,000 killed and wounded.
Confederate losses were nearly as great—but
these men could not be replaced. Sherman was
able to draw from the Union's seemingly
inexhaustible supply of young men.

Union General William
Tecumseh Sherman led the
march through Georgia.

Grant's first encounter with Lee's army was in
an area of Virginia called the Wilderness—a
region of dense underbrush, forests, and swamps.
Lee's men knew the Wilderness, the scene of
Stonewall Jackson's famous flanking maneuver at

85

Sherman's men destroy a section of railroad in Georgia.

Chancellorsville. This time, the two armies fought blindly in the dense undergrowth where battle smoke made the air even more impenetrable. The Union forces took a severe beating, suffering 17,000 casualties, many of the men were killed in a fire sparked by gunfire. Confederate losses were barely half that number. In this new phase of the war, however, the South lost strength because they had no replacements.

The Federals emerged from the Wilderness with a sense of futility. According to the way the Army of the Potomac had fought every battle in their efforts to take Richmond, the army would now

86

retreat, lick its wounds, regroup, and eventually try again. Instead of retreating, however, Grant made it clear that he was moving forward. This restored the Federal army's morale. They had never been led by a general like Grant.

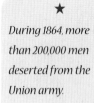

Having been beaten in the Wilderness by Lee, Grant tried a flanking maneuver and sent his men on a race to a crossroads called Spotsylvania Court House. When they arrived, they found the Confederates already there—Lee had guessed the move and headed it off. The war changed at this point because the Rebels were dug in behind strong entrenchments—outer defenses they had built earlier for the defense of Richmond. A Union officer wrote, "The great feature of this campaign is the extraordinary use of earthworks. When our line advances, there is the line of the enemy, nothing showing but the bayonets, and the battle flags stuck on top of the works."

In the Spotsylvania battle of May 9 through 12, 1864, Grant tried to have his men force their way through a V-shaped salient in the Confederate lines, called the "Bloody Angle." The two sides stood within 50 feet of each other, blasting away relentlessly. The bullets flew so thick that an oak tree 23 inches in diameter was shredded to fiber and bodies were shot to pieces—one was found with 80 bullet holes.

Having been blocked by the Confederates at Spotsylvania Court House, Grant maneuvered to his left once again, this time to Cold Harbor, and there, in May, 1864, made his last attempt to crush Lee's army with frontal assaults. In one futile charge, Lee's men cut down 7,000 Federals in less than thirty minutes—the deadliest rate of casualties of the war.

Grant finally decided he would have to resort to siege warfare as he had done at Vicksburg. His Army of the Potomac had suffered 55,000 casualties in what would be the bloodiest month in any American war. Northern newspapers were beginning to call him "the Butcher," and one supporter said, "the army has literally marched in blood and agony from the Rapidan [River] to the James [River]."

Lee's casualties numbered 32,000 out of his original 65,000. He did manage to find some replacements, but it was clear that this rate of loss would eventually destroy the Army of Northern Virginia. Grant's next move was to bypass Richmond and head for Petersburg, the last rail center that could supply Lee's army. The Rebel soldiers headed for the trenches already prepared around Petersburg. They knew the end was near, but they were not ready to give up. One Confederate veteran wrote about his comrades:

> *"Instead of growling and deserting, they laughed at their own bare feet, ragged clothes and pinched faces; and weak, hungry, cold, wet, worried with vermin and*

itch, dirty, with no hope of reward or rest, they marched cheerfully to meet the . . . enemy.

In time, the siege of Petersburg turned into a nightmare. Grant and Meade had a huge supply depot built on the James River and a railroad line to carry food, clothing, and ammunition to the army. From the Union lines, it looked as though the ragged Confederates could not put up any kind of a fight. Every time the Federals tried to break through, however, the Rebels drove them back ferociously.

Union General Philip Sheridan

The siege continued into the winter of 1865. In the meantime, the South was losing on every other front. During this time, Sherman had burned Atlanta to the ground and started his "March to the Sea," cutting a 60-mile-wide path of destruction across Georgia to the coast. Sherman's men, followed by throngs of happy freed slaves, left nothing that could be of any use to the enemy. It was said that a crow flying across Georgia would have to carry its own rations. In the Shenandoah Valley, General Philip Sheridan's cavalry was nearly as efficient in destroying the autumn harvest.

By March 1865, Lee's army had little left to fight with. The entire Confederacy now had only about 65,000 soldiers left. The roughly 15,000

89

The Finest Hours

When Grant's final campaign against Robert E. Lee is assessed, he is often faulted for battle strategies that resulted in enormous loss of life for troops under his command. Though there is little question that Grant's tactics could not measure up against those of Robert E. Lee, the role played by both men in bringing the war to an end at Appomattox Court House is often overlooked. Few people realize how close our nation came to fighting a war that could have lasted for decades rather than just four terrible years.

Even on April 8, the day before Lee's surrender, the Confederates—outnumbered six to one, sick and starving—were not ready to give in. Lee, in fact, planned to send his men on a surprise attack to break through Union lines. Led by General John Gordon, the Rebels then planned to head for the Blue Ridge Mountains where they could hold out "for twenty years."

As the sun rose on April 9, the Rebels attacked, driving back Federal cavalry and capturing several cannons. Reaching the crest of a hill, however, Gordon, and finally Lee, realized what they were up against. A solid wall of Union soldiers two miles wide was advancing toward them. There was no choice but for Lee to surrender his men. There would be no guerilla war, he said. There had been enough bloodshed.

Tormented by migraine headaches and insomnia, Grant himself had been up since 4 A.M. When Lee's offer of surrender reached him, Grant made a small gesture that showed his intentions toward the defeated Rebels: He allowed Lee to choose the time and place for surrender. The vanquished, not the victor, would set the stage.

Thus, in early afternoon, Grant and Lee met in the McLean house in the village of Appomattox Court House. Ironically, the home's owner, Wilmer McLean, had moved there after his home in Manassas had been destroyed in the first Battle of Bull Run.

At 1:30 P.M., Lee rode in on Traveller in a spotless gray dress uniform. Grant rode in moments later in his mud-spattered boots and half-buttoned private's shirt, having already written out generous terms. At first he appeared awe-struck in the presence of the great Robert E. Lee, chatting nervously until Lee reminded him of the purpose of their meeting. Despite his nerves, his ragged appearance, and his reputation, Grant was now about take on his most important role—statesman.

Sitting at separate tables, Lee listened, almost stunned, as Grant's aide read the terms of surrender. There would be no prison, no parade of captured Confederates down Washington's streets, no charges of treason. Confederate officers could keep their side arms and horses. The men only had to turn over their rifles and sign a parole agreeing not to fight again.

Lee, shocked by the generous terms, thanked Grant, saying, "This will do much toward conciliating our people." Then Lee asked Grant about the many Union prisoners he still held. He could not feed them. "Indeed, I have nothing for my own men," Lee said. Without hesitation, Grant offered to send 25,000 rations across the lines. Was that enough, he wondered? "An abundance, I assure you," replied Lee.

Soon, the sound of cheering spread through Union lines. Grant ordered the celebration to stop. As he watched Lee ride back to Rebel lines their eyes met. Grant simply lifted his hat in a sign of respect to the great general. Lee, in return, tipped his own hat. As he rode away, Federal officers along the way followed Grant's example and tipped their hats. For the dignified loser and the gracious winner, those were the finest hours of the terrible war.

An illustration of Appomattox Court House, Virginia.

men with Lee were half-starved when he gave the order to abandon Petersburg on April 2. The Confederate government fled Richmond after setting the warehouses ablaze. Lee seemed to have some desperate hope of reaching the remnants of Joe Johnston's force.

Despite his terrible situation, Lee stubbornly refused to surrender. "Surrender?" he echoed when his generals suggested it. "I have too many good fighting men for that!"

Robert E. Lee

In the first week of April after failure to get re-supplied at Amelia, Lee knew the end was near for his troops. He could ask no more of his army. Now totally surrounded by Union troops, Lee agreed to talk with Grant at Appomattox Court House. But he also allowed Generals Gordon and Longstreet to try one last breakout that failed in minutes. "There is nothing left for me but to go and see General Grant," Lee said finally, "and I would rather face a thousand deaths."

93

Grant and Lee met in the McLean house in the little village of Appomattox Court House at 1:30 P.M. on April 9, 1865—a scene that instantly became part of American folklore. Lee appeared in a splendid gray uniform, complete with sash and a jewel-studded dress sword. Grant arrived in his well-worn uniform, and half-buttoned private's shirt. The Confederate officers could keep their side arms and horses. The men only had to surrender their rifles and agree not to fight again. Lee thanked him, saying, "This will do much toward conciliating our people." As he left, Lee shook hands with Grant's assistant, Ely Parker, a Seneca Indian. Noting Parker's Native American features, Lee said, "I am glad to see one real American here." Parker replied, "We are all Americans, sir."

Cheering spread through the Union lines, and the cannons began firing. The men shouted, hugged each other, jumped up and down, delirious with joy. Grant ordered the celebrations to stop. "The war is over," he said. "The rebels are our countrymen again."

Lee, meanwhile faced the task of telling his own troops that the Army of Northern Virginia was no more. Troops who saw him ride by did not need to be told what had happened. Tears streaked the General's cheeks. But Lee was as determined to do as much to reunite North and South as he had been to tear it apart. He turned to his men, many of whom were sobbing. "Boys, go home now," Lee said. "and if you make as good citizens as you have soldiers, you will do well, and I shall always be proud of you."

The formal surrender took place on April 12, with Union General Joshua Chamberlain, the hero of Little Round Top, chosen to accept the surrender from Lee's appointee, General John Gordon. As the tattered gray ranks marched forward, still carrying their shredded battle flags, Chamberlain ordered Union troops to shift from "order arms" to the "marching salute," the highest honor military men can give to other military men. General Gordon, riding at the head of the Rebel column heard the hands slapping on muskets and understood the gesture. He instantly wheeled his horse upright, dipped the point of his sword and ordered his men to return the salute. General Chamberlain recorded the solemn moment:

Confederate General John Gordon

> "It was honor answering honor. On our part not a sound of trumpet more, nor roll of drum; not a cheer, nor word nor whisper of vaingloring, nor motion of man standing again at the order, but an awed stillness rather, and breath-holding, as if it were the passing of the dead."

95

POSTSCRIPT

THE LAST YEARS

At the time of the surrender, General Lee and many of his officers expected that they would be taken prisoner and probably be put on trial for treason. They were relieved by Grant's generous terms, and Lee was given a pass so that he could go through Union lines.

But where would he go? He met Mary at Richmond, and friends found them a small house. President Lincoln was assassinated on April 14, two days after the formal surrender. Many in the Republican government, eager to avenge the murder—and the war—imposed harsh policies on the defeated South. In June 1865, Lee was indicted for treason and many expected that a trial would be followed by execution. Through a mutual friend, Lee quietly sought Grant's help.

★

Grant and his wife were supposed to accompany the Lincolns to Ford's Theater on April 14, but cancelled at the last minute.

★

Grant agreed to help and angrily threatened to resign his position as only the second full general since George Washington, if Lee was arrested. The treason indictment was dropped and Lee was not troubled again, although the government refused to restore his citizenship.

Robert E. Lee lived only five years after the war's end. He became president of Washington College in Lexington, Virginia, a small college with forty students and four professors, in

September 1865. It gave him a position from which he could urge all Southerners to accept the restoration of the Union. The college later became Washington and Lee University.

Although he tried various cures for his heart disease, including trips to White Sulphur Springs, Virginia, nothing helped. He died of a stroke on October 12, 1870, at the age of sixty-three.

In trying to assess the greatness of Robert E. Lee, the mythical figure repeatedly gets in the way. In the years after the Civil War, biographies of him were written mainly by Southerners. These books, not surprisingly, presented Lee as a god-like figure who could do no wrong on the battlefield or off it.

More recent books about Lee have presented a more balanced view, but it is still hard to gain a truly accurate picture. Most historians regard his abilities on the battlefield against numerical superiority as extraordinary. Even in the last months, when Grant's overwhelming numbers were wearing down Lee's army, he could turn and snap back.

It could also be said, however, that both Lee and Grant became somewhat reckless in their expenditure of human lives to achieve a victory. Any battle, of course, forces a general to steel himself to the suffering and death of his own men. Grant, in fact, would whittle a piece of wood during battle to distract himself from the carnage. But there were times when Lee's

Robert E. Lee sits astride his horse, Traveller.

determination to win led him to throw caution to the winds. This was most evident at Gettysburg, where on the last day he seemed to convince himself that Pickett's charge could succeed.

To try to find a balance in assessing Lee's life and career, it is important to consider his brave humanity. That humanity was demonstrated as the war ended when Lee refused recommendations from President Jefferson Davis and others that Southern troops be dispersed into the countryside to continue a guerilla war against the Union. Such a course, Lee knew, might have prolonged the war for a generation. Lee had seen enough of death and destruction in his native state and across the South. He accepted the defeat and devoted his energy toward reuniting the South and the North.

Perhaps one final scene captures Lee at his finest. In a church in Richmond, late in 1865, a priest called worshipers forward to receive communion. Suddenly a well-dressed African American came down the center aisle and knelt before the priest. White worshipers were shocked. In years past, African Americans sat off to the side and only took communion when all the whites were finished.

The priest froze, uncertain how to proceed. White worshipers remained in their seats, unwilling to come forward and kneel beside a person whose people had once been at the bottom of Southern society.

As the awkward discomfort spread across the church, a bearded, gray-haired white man stood and slowly walked up the aisle. He looked exhausted and much older than the newspaper images. As the man stopped and knelt beside the African American, he seemed to send a message to fellow Southerners: Life had changed forever in the South, and it was time to forget the past. That man kneeling at the altar was, of course, Robert E. Lee.

Glossary

artillery Large weapons used by fighting forces that fall into three categories-guns or cannons, howitzers, and mortars

brigade A military unit smaller that a division, usually consisting of three to five regiments of 500 to 1,000 soldiers

earthworks Holes, pits, or trenches dug for defensive stands by armies

casualties The total number of soldiers dead, wounded, and missing after a battles

commander A military leader, usually holding the rank of general

corps A military grouping of between 10,000 and 20,000 soldiers

division A military grouping of between 6,000 and 8,000 soldiers or two to three brigades

emancipation Freedom

flotilla A small fleet of ships

ford A crossing on a stream or river.

plantation A large farm in the South worked by slaves in the years before the war

regiment A military unit smaller than brigade and a division. In the Civil War soldiers fought in the same regiment throughout the war with fellow soldiers who usually from the same state, city, or town

reinforce In military terms, to send strengthen a military unit by sending in fresh troops

secede To break away

siege The surrounding and blockading of a city, town, or fortress by an army attempting to capture it

skirmishes Minor or preliminary conflicts or disputes

typhoid An often-fatal disease caused by contaminated drinking water

101

For More Information

Web Sites

Robert Edward Lee (1807-1870)
http://www.civilwarhome.com/leebio.htm
A brief biography with links to other information and some of Lee's original writing,

Stratford Hall Plantation: Birthplace of Robert E. Lee
http://www.stratfordhall.org/history.htm
Good site for historical background on the Lee family and early Virginia

Robert E Lee
http://www.norfacad.pvt.k12.va.us/project/lee/lee.htm
Student-created web site with biography separated into early middle and late years

U.S. Civil War Photos: Robert E. Lee
http://usa-civil-war.com/Lee/lee.html
Brief biography accompanied by many photos of Lee and the battlefields on which his men fought.

Books

Archer, Jules. *A House Divided: Ulysses Grant and Robert E Lee.* New York, Scholastic 1994. A book that examines the path each man took leading to Appomattox.

Cannon, Marian. *Robert E. Lee: Defender of the South.* (First Books) New York. Franklin Watts, 1993.

Kavanaugh, Jack & Murdoch, Eugene. *Robert E. Lee: Civil War Hero.* (Junior World Biography Series) New York: Chelsea House, 1994.

Index

Robert E. Lee